Midnight Rituals: A Guide to the World's Scariest Rituals and Haunting Games

SIRIUS H. DREAMWALKER

DEDICATION

To my love, my regret — always waiting for you.

CONTENTS

ACKNOWLEDGMENTS

In the dim light of knowledge sought and secrets unearthed, this book stands as a testament to the mysteries that both beckon and beguile. My journey into the shadowy realms of the world's most haunting rituals and games was as perilous as it was profound, and it is with a solemn heart that I offer these findings to you.

I extend my deepest gratitude to those brave souls whose whispered tales filled these pages—without their courage, this compilation would not exist. To my readers, I entrust this guide: may it illuminate your path with caution and curiosity. Venture wisely, for the veil is thin and easily torn.

As I pen this final note, the shadows lengthen and the air grows thin. The call of the unknown grows louder, its pull irresistible. I am drawn to a reunion with my lost love, separated by time and fate, now waiting beyond the veil. This book is my last gift, my final echo in the mortal realm.

Tread lightly, dear reader, for we may not meet again.

INTRODUCTION

Beneath the cloak of midnight, when the world quiets and shadows swell, lies the threshold to realms untold, whispering secrets of the night. "Midnight Rituals: A Guide to the World's Scariest Rituals and Haunting Games" emerges as a beacon into this darkness, an invitation to the curious and the bold to step beyond the mundane and peer into the abyss of the paranormal. This tome is not merely a collection; it is a passage through the veil, a journey into the heart of darkness where the most chilling rituals and games await those daring enough to try them.

Within these pages lie the instructions and tales of ten eerie ceremonies, each more haunting than the last. From the nerve-racking suspense of "The Midnight Game" to the eerie solitude of "One-Man Hide and Seek", this guide traverses the spectrum of the supernatural. You will summon spirits in the reflective depths of "Bloody Mary", ascend through dimensions in "The Elevator Game", and traverse the lonely expanse of "11 Miles".

Dare to invite the unknown into your home with "The Hosting Game", or court the whispers of the night in "The Dark Music Ritual". "The Clock and Candles Game" will challenge your perception of time and reality, while "The Three Wishes Ritual" offers a glimpse into the power of desire—and its price. And should you seek to know your fate, "Tsuji-ura" awaits at the crossroads, where the future is whispered by strangers.

"Midnight Rituals" serves as both guide and warning, for these games are not for the faint of heart. They tread the line between our world and the darkness beyond, inviting forces unseen and perhaps better left undisturbed. Yet, for those who seek to uncover the mysteries that lie in the shadowed corners of our existence, this book is a key to unlocking doors for which no keys should exist.

So, dear reader, as you delve into the mysteries contained within these pages, remember: the world of the paranormal is vast and unknowable, and the rituals and games you are about to explore are as dangerous as they are enticing. Tread carefully, for the darkness you invite in may not so easily be dispelled

THE MIDNIGHT GAME

The Midnight Game is believed to be an ancient Pagan ritual, initially used as a punishment for those who dared to violate the sacred laws. While once a tool for spiritual enforcement, today it is played for thrill and intrigue, a dangerous beckoning into the supernatural that is not for the faint of heart.

It is highly recommended that you DO NOT PLAY THE MIDNIGHT GAME.

Prerequisites

The rite must be performed at exactly 12:00 AM.
Otherwise, it will not work.

Requirements

- A piece of paper and a writing implement.
- At least one drop of your own blood.
- A candle and a lighter or matches.
- A wooden door, closed.
- A timer or clock.
- Salt.

Warnings and Considerations

- Do not switch on any lights during the Midnight Game.
- Do not use a flashlight during the Midnight Game.
- Do not fall asleep during the Midnight Game.
- Do not try to use another person's blood in your name.
- Do not use a lighter instead of a candle. It won't work.
- Do not, under any circumstances, attempt to provoke the Midnight Man.
- Even when the game is finished, he will still be watching you...
- Good luck; you will need it.

Step 1

Write your full name (first, middle, and last) on the piece of paper.

Add at least one drop of your blood on the same paper.

Step 2

Turn off all the lights in your home.

Place the paper with your name and blood in front of the wooden door.

Light the candle and place it on top of the paper.

Step 3

Knock on the door 22 times with the final knock timed to occur at exactly midnight.

Open the door, blow out the candle, and then close the door again.

You have just allowed the "Midnight Man" to enter your house.

Step 4

Immediately relight your candle.
This is where the game begins.

You must now lurk around your now-completely dark house, holding the lit candle in your hand. The goal is to avoid the Midnight Man at all means till 3:33 AM.

If your candle goes out, it indicates the Midnight Man is near you.

It's necessary to relight your candle within the next 10 seconds.

If you are unsuccessful in doing so, you must immediately surround yourself with a circle of salt. If you fail in both of your activities, the Midnight Man will create a hallucination of your worst fear and take out your organs one at a time. You will feel it yet be unable to react.

If you are successful in forming the circle of salt, you must stay there until 3:33 AM.

If you succeed in relighting your candle, you can continue with the game.

Step 5

To win the Midnight Game, you must survive until 3:33 AM without being attacked by the Midnight Man or trapped inside the salt circle.

The Midnight Man will leave your home at 3:33 AM, and you will be safe to continue with your morning.

Addition

A dramatic drop in temperature, seeing a pure black, humanoid figure in the darkness, and hearing very soft whispers from an indiscernible source are all indications that you are near the Midnight Man.

If you encounter any of them, it is recommended that you leave the area to avoid the Midnight Man.

ONE-MAN HIDE AND SEEK

One-Man Hide and Seek, also known as "Hitori Kakurenbo," is a ritual that invokes the presence of spirits using a doll as a vessel. It's a game that originated in Japan, mixing elements of spiritualism with the adrenaline rush of hide and seek. This game is not just a test of bravery; it's a communion with the otherworldly.

This game involves significant risk, not only of psychological distress but also of unwanted spiritual attention. Players have reported unexplained phenomena and lingering presences long after the game has concluded.

Prerequisites

The rite must begin at exactly 3:00 AM.
Otherwise, it will not work.

Requirements

- A stuffed doll with limbs.
- Rice, enough to fill the doll.
- A needle and crimson thread.
- A pair of nail clippers.
- A sharp-edged tool, like a knife or scissors.
- A cup of salt water.
- A bathroom, with a bathtub.
- A hiding place.

Warnings and Considerations

- Do not leave the house until you have completed the ritual.
- When instructed, you must turn off all lights in your home.
- You must remain silent while hiding.
- You do not need to put the salt water in your mouth during the beginning stages. You just need to do it during the final rite.
- Keep in mind that if you live with someone, you might put them in danger too.
- If the ritual lasts longer than two hours, the spirit will become too powerful to be expelled.
- It could be advisable to leave all of the doors in the house unlocked, including the front door, for safety reasons. Also, have friends close by so that they can help you at any time. Additionally, it might be a good idea to keep a cell phone nearby.
- Please never interrupt the ritual halfway. You have to follow it through to the end.

Step 1

Cut open the doll, remove the stuffing, and fill it with rice.

Clip a piece of your fingernail and place it inside the doll, which binds the doll to you.

Sew the doll up with the crimson thread, then tie the remaining thread around the doll.

Fill the bathtub with water.

Give your doll a name.

Step 2

Now the time should be 3 AM.

Say to the doll, *"[Your name] is the first it"*, three times to signify the beginning of the game.

Place the doll in the bathtub.

Turn off all lights in your home, go to your hiding place, and switch on the television.

Step 3

Close your eyes and count to ten.

After that, return to the bathroom with the edged tool in your hand.

Say, *"I have found you, [doll's name]"*, and then use the edged tool to cut the crimson thread binding the doll. This signifies that you have found the doll.

Step 4

Say, *"Now, [doll's name] is it"*, and leave the doll on the counter in the bathroom.

As soon as you have put the doll down, run back to the hiding place, and hide.

The goal is to not get found by the doll, which now seeks you.

Step 5

When you wish to end the game, take a mouthful of salt water, and then find the doll.

Do not drink it, just keep it there.

Keep the cup containing the rest of the salt water in your hand.

The doll may not be in the bathroom where you left it.

Step 6

When you find the doll, pour the rest of the salt water in the cup over it.

Then spit the salt water in your mouth onto it as well.

Say, *"I win"*, three times.

Step 7

Once the game has been completed, allow the doll to dry.

Then burn it and discard the remains.

Addition

Never leave your hiding place without the salt water if you notice abnormal behavior.

Once the ritual has been started, the game must be played through to completion.

BLOODY MARY

The Bloody Mary ritual is a dark and haunting game that challenges the bravest souls to summon a ghostly apparition in a mirror. Rooted deeply in folklore, this ritual is often played by those seeking a thrill, yet the outcomes can be unpredictably terrifying.

Prerequisites

Use a candle if possible.

Requirements

- A dark room with a mirror.
- A candle or a flashlight for minimal illumination.

Warnings and Considerations

- Participants have reported experiencing psychological distress and haunting phenomena long after the ritual has ended.

Step 1

Enter the room where the ritual will take place.
This is typically a bathroom.

Turn off the lights and draw the curtains to ensure the
room is as dark as possible.

Step 2

Light the candle or turn on the flashlight.

The light source should provide just enough light to see
your reflection in the mirror.

Step 3

Stand in front of the mirror, holding the light source, and
stare into your reflection.

Step 4

Clearly and audibly, repeat the name *"Bloody Mary"* three
times.

Step 5

After calling her name, wait and watch in the mirror.

According to the legend, an apparition of Bloody Mary should appear in the mirror.

Step 6

To conclude, simply turn on the lights and leave the room.

The ritual doesn't specify a particular way to end the encounter beyond this.

THE ELEVATOR GAME

Originating from Korea, The Elevator Game is a chilling ritual purported to access another world. Players must use an elevator in a specific sequence to allegedly cross over into a parallel dimension. The game combines urban legend with supernatural risk, creating an eerie atmosphere for thrill-seekers.

Prerequisites

If you bring anyone else along with you, the ritual will not work.

Requirements

- A building with at least 10 floors and an elevator that you can use undisturbed.
- You must be the only person performing this ritual.
- Mental preparation for the journey you're about to undertake.

Warnings and Considerations

- DO NOT LOOK AT HER. DO NOT SPEAK TO HER. DO NOT TOUCH HER.
- The sequence is 4-2-6-2-10-5-1.

Step 1

Enter your chosen building.

Enter the elevator from the ground floor alone.

Step 2

Begin the sequence by pressing the button for the 4th floor.

If anyone gets on the elevator, stop the ritual.

Step 3

After reaching the 4th floor, press the button for the 2nd floor.

Do not get out.

If anyone gets on the elevator, stop the ritual.

Step 4

When you arrive at the 2nd floor, proceed by pressing the button for the 6th floor.

Do not get out.

If anyone gets on the elevator, stop the ritual.

Step 5

Upon reaching the 6th floor, select the 2nd floor again.

Do not get out.

If anyone gets on the elevator, stop the ritual.

Step 6

Once back at the 2nd floor, ascend to the 10th floor.

Do not get out.

If anyone gets on the elevator, stop the ritual.

Step 7

From the 10th floor, make your final selection for the 5th floor.

Do not get out.

If anyone gets on the elevator, stop the ritual.

Step 8

On the 5th floor, a woman may enter the elevator.

DO NOT LOOK AT HER. DO NOT SPEAK TO HER. DO NOT TOUCH HER.

This entity is not what she seems; speaking to or looking at her could have dire consequences.

Step 9

Press the button for the 1st floor.

If it descends to the 1st floor, you must exit immediately upon opening, without looking back or speaking. You can try the ritual again, but don't do it in the same elevator anymore.

If instead of descending, the elevator begins to ascend to the 10th floor, you may proceed.

This is your last chance to stop the ritual.

To end this ritual, press the button for the first floor before the elevator passes the ninth floor. Once you reach the first floor, leave the building without comment and do not look back.

Step 10

If the elevator reaches the 10th floor, the doors will open.

You have the choice to either remain in the elevator or step out into the other world.

The other world appears similar to ours but is devoid of life; no one except you will be seen

How to exit the alternate reality

Step 11

If you choose to stay aboard the elevator:

Press the button for the first floor.

Once you have reached the first floor, leave the building and do not look back.

Step 12

If you choose to leave the elevator you must use the same elevator to descend.

Press the buttons in the same sequence: 4-2-6-2-10-5.

Then press the button for the 1st floor to return to our world.

Step 13

If the elevator again ascends to the 10th floor, press any other floor's button to cancel the ascent.

You must keep pressing until the elevator begins to move to a different floor.

Step 14

Once you have reached the first floor, do not get out just yet.

Take a peek around the area surrounding the elevator. Are there people?

If so, are they reacting normally? Is anything out of place?

If you believe you have not returned to normal reality, repeat Steps 12-13, until you are certain you have left the Otherworld.

Step 15

If you believe you are back in our reality, exit the building and head home immediately and don't look back.

Don't say anything.

Addition

If you have been incorrect about your judgment and have decided to leave the elevator, it's over.

You will probably stay in the Otherworld forever.

Make sure you keep this book with you as a guide, as electronic devices may not work.

11 MILES

The 11 Miles ritual is an obscure and mystical challenge rumored to fulfill the deepest desires of those who dare to complete it. Participants must drive through an eerie, seldom-traveled road where each mile tests their resolve, courage, and sanity.

Prerequisites

Make sure your vehicle is reliable and doesn't break in the middle of this ritual.

Dress up warmly; it'll be cold.

Requirements

- A vehicle, preferably one you are comfortable driving for an extended period.
- A secluded, rural road that stretches uninterrupted for at least 11 miles.
- A deep wish or desire.
- Mental preparation for facing potential psychological stress.

Warnings and Considerations

- Do not turn on the radio, CD player, mp3 player or other music devices.
- Do not use a cell phone.
- Do not open the windows.
- Do not drive faster than 30 miles per hour.
- Do not leave the car.
- Keep your eyes on the road.
- Buckle up.

Step 1

Begin the ritual close to midnight for the best chance of completing it.

Drive to the woods. The woods must be a particular type of woods.

The road you take to them must also pass through them.

Drive and begin looking.

Let your wish guide you.

You will know the road when you see it.

Step 2

When you are certain you have located the road, take a moment if you need it.

You may stop the car if you wish.

Proceed only when you are ready.

Drive.

Step 3

Mile 1: It gets cold. You should turn your heater on.

The journey begins with a sense of unease, a whisper in the dark that something has changed. The air feels denser, heavier, as if charged with a silent anticipation. The world beyond the headlights seems to recede into an impenetrable darkness.

Mile 2: Turn on the heater or you will regret it later.

A chill creeps through the air, seeping into bones and souls alike. It's not just the cold; it's a feeling of being watched, of unseen eyes boring into the very essence of those who dare this path. The first whispers of doubt may begin to surface.

Mile 3: Ignore any shadows in the trees. They are not humans.

The darkness grows oppressive, thick with unspoken horrors. Shadows seem to move of their own accord, darting just out of sight. The sound of the engine becomes a distant echo, as if the car and its occupant are moving through another world entirely.

Mile 4: Ignore any voices you hear. They are not from humans.

Unexplained phenomena begin. Maybe it's a flicker of movement in the rearview mirror, or a sudden drop in temperature, chilling the breath. The line between the real and the unreal blurs, the mind struggling to grasp at the fraying edges of logic.

Mile 5: Ignore the vanishing of the trees, sudden appearance of a lake, and the glowing of the moon.

The air is filled with the sound of whispers, voices that seem both far away and uncomfortably close. They speak in tongues unknown, a cacophony of the damned that frays the nerves and tests the spirit.

Mile 6: Ignore the reappearance of the trees. Ignore the flickering of your headlights.

Your radio might turn on. Do not touch the radio. Just ignore it all.

Visions plague the journey now, terrifying in their intensity. Forms appear in the darkness, grotesque and twisted, their eyes glowing with malice. They vanish as quickly as they come, leaving only the pounding heart as evidence of their presence.

Mile 7: Ignore—again—every voice you hear, no matter how close or humane they may sound. Do not turn around. Do not look at the backseat.

The world itself seems to turn against the traveler. The road twists in impossible ways, the landscape warping into nightmarish visions. Reality is a concept left far behind, lost in the darkness of the road.

Mile 8: Slow down, but do not stop. Break if your headlight flickers, but never stop your vehicle. No matter how cold it is, do not stop. No matter what, don't stop.

Despair sets in, a crushing weight that threatens to smother all hope. Memories, dark and twisted, surface unbidden, playing on the deepest fears and regrets. It is a mile of psychological torment, a test of inner strength.

Mile 9: Your vehicle might stall. Close your eyes immediately and restart your vehicle.

No matter what, do not open your eyes and keep trying to start your vehicle.

When your vehicle starts, hit the gas as fast as you can. When the mile is over, you may open your eyes.

The air is thick with the scent of death, a stench that clings to the soul. The sounds of the unseen horrors grow louder, a symphony of nightmares that seeks to overwhelm the senses.

Mile 10: Do not look in your rear-view mirror.

Here, at the penultimate stretch, the very fabric of existence seems to tear. The veil between worlds is at its thinnest, the darkness pulsating with unseen energy. It is a place where reality bends, and the impossible becomes possible.

Mile 11: Your vehicle loses power, but keeps moving. Let it.

If you see a red light ahead, close your eyes immediately. Close them tightly.

Cover your ears if you can. Make sure you can't see anything. Make sure you can't hear anything.

No matter what you might hear. DO NOT LOOK.

No matter what you might feel. DO NOT LOOK.

No matter how hot it gets. DO NOT LOOK.

When the power returns, stop your vehicle. You can open your eyes now.

Take a breath. Take a moment, and drive.

And then, silence. A profound, deafening silence that envelops everything. The road stretches out, leading to the final choice. Here, the deepest desires can be whispered into the void, offered up to the darkness. But beware, for the road demands its price, and the cost of one's desires may be more than they are willing to pay.

Step 4

Drive until the road dead ends. Stop.

Close your eyes and relax.

Step 5

Imagine your deepest desire, your greatest aspiration, innermost craving.

Even if it has changed from what it was initially, imagine it all the same – changes and all.

Imagine possessing it, not just desiring it.

Step 6

Open your eyes.

If your desire was an object, check your trunk, backseat, or pocket, depending on the size of the object.

If your desire was non-material, return home and keep living your life. It will eventually appear in your life. Be patient.

Addition

You might have returned to the start of the road where you initially started the journey.

Will you return home or begin the journey again?

The choice is yours.

THE HOSTING GAME

The Hosting Game involves inviting unseen entities into your home. This chilling ritual tests the boundaries between the known and the unknown, allowing participants a glimpse into the paranormal.

This game can result in prolonged paranormal activity in your home. Participants often report unexplained disturbances and feelings of being watched long after the game has concluded. Extreme caution and preparation are advised.

Prerequisites

The game should be played at night time. Preferable after midnight.

Requirements

- A quiet, empty room in your home, referred to as the "hosting room."
- A pencil and a piece of paper.
- Three matches.
- A clock or a watch. Analog timekeeping device. Not digital.
- A candle or candles.
- Courage and a steady heart.

Warnings and Considerations

- Do not assume that your guests have gone even after ending the ritual.
- Avoid dark rooms in your home even after performing a purifying ritual.

Step 1

Make sure all possible sources of noise are turned off.

Draw curtains or block the windows by other means to make sure any light cannot cast to the room.

Step 2

Enter your hosting room and light candle(s).

Place your pencil and sheet of paper in your hosting room.

Step 3

Exist the hosting room and leave the candles lit.

Go to the furthest point in your home from the room and call the guests:

"I'll be ready soon!".

Move from room to room repeating the invitation while moving closer to your hosting room with each call.

Step 4

Last, go back to your hosting room and write to the piece of paper the following:

*"You are invited! A gathering, hosted by **[your name]**. Take place from **[the current time]** to **[an hour from the current time]**. Bring your friends!"*

Place the paper in the middle of the room.

Step 5

Go to the doorway of the hosting room and while facing into the room say,

"I'm ready! Come on in!"

Blow out the candle(s) and turn around.

You should be facing away from the hosting room now.

Step 6

Take out your three matches.

Start counting from one to ten aloud.

Step 7

When you reach the 10, strike the first match.

If the first match light on the first try:

Hold it as it burns down and greet your guests saying,

"I'm so glad to see you! Thank you for coming!"

When you can't bear the heat, drop it.

If the first match does not light on the first try:

Drop it and continue to the next step.

Step 8

Strike the second match.

If the second match light on the first try:

Hold it as it burns down and greet more of your guests saying,

"I'm so glad to see you! Thank you for coming!"

When you can't bear the heat, drop it.

If the second match does not light on the first try:

Drop it and continue to the next step.

Step 9

Strike the third match.

If the third match light on the first try:

Say *"Now everyone is here!"* and start counting from one to ten.

Now you should be able to hear whispering and rustling behind you.

Do not look back.

When your analog timekeeping device indicates the finishing time, say

"Thank you for coming. Goodbye."

Walk to the nearest light source and turn it on to finish the ritual.

If the third match does not light on the first try:

You have uninvited guests, and it's bad.

Run immediately to the nearest light source and turn it on without looking back.

Addition

It is recommended to perform a cleansing ritual and avoid dark corners of your home from now on.

THE DARK MUSIC RITUAL

The Dark Music Ritual is a profound and disturbing game that taps into the depths of the human psyche through music played in utter darkness. This ritual allows participants to confront their innermost fears and desires, manifested through haunting melodies.

Prerequisites

The ritual should be played in a pitch-black room.

Requirements

- A dark room with a door.
- A musical instrument.
- A needle.
- A cup.
- A pencil.
- A sheet of paper.
- A container of salt.
- A cup of salt water.
- A hiding place.

Warnings and Considerations

- Do not stand between the instrument and the door.
- Always have your cup of salt water.

MIDNIGHT RITUALS

Step 1

Turn off all the lights and begin at night.

Place the instrument in front of the door inside the room.

Do not stand between the door and the instrument.

Step 2

With the needle, poke the part of your body that is typically used to play the instrument you chose.

Deposit a drop of blood on the area of the instrument that part of your body would touch in order to play.

If you chose the piano, prick your finger and deposit a drop of blood on the keys.

Step 3

Write a short message on the sheet of paper, asking the spirit to play you a song.

Use polite wording.

Place the note next to the instrument.

Step 4

Draw a line of salt between you and the instrument.

Step 5

Go to your hiding place with the salt and salt water.

Your hiding place needs to be hidden from the instrument.

Step 6

Sit still and be silent.

Listen the music.

Step 7

When the music stops you can leave your hiding place.

Take the salt water with you and go to the line of salt.

Step 8

If the line of salt or the instrument is broken, jump immediately to step 13.

If not, you may proceed to step 9.

Step 9

With both hands cut the line of salt from the middle.

Go to the instrument, but don't stand between the instrument and the door.

Step 10

Pick up the note and fold it three times.

Put the folded note into the cup of salt water.

Put the salt water cup next to the instrument where the note previously was

Step 11

Politely thank the spirit for its performance.

Use the salt water to clean the blood from the instrument.

Step 12

Ritual is over and you should go to sleep.

Don't make too much noise or play any music.

Step 13

Follow these steps only if something goes wrong with the ritual or instructed.

For example, music plays out of tune or goes into sudden halt

Step 14

Quickly go to the instrument with the salt water.

Splash half of the salt water on the floor between the door and the instrument.

Do not stand between the door and the instrument.

After this you have 15 seconds

Step 15

Pick up the note and tear it into five pieces.

Crumple each piece and put it into the salt water cup.

Make sure all the pieces are soaked.

Step 16

Ask the spirit for forgiveness.

Ask the spirit for forgiveness.

Ask the spirit for forgiveness.

Step 17

Pick up the instrument and play it for 10 seconds.

Keep it simple and clean.

Do not play the same music as the spirit.

Step 18

If you managed to follow all the steps you might survive the night.

If not, well then…

Step 19

Put down the instrument and turn on the lights.

Be still and wait for an hour to pass.

Make a new cup of salt water and clean the blood from the instrument.

Never play music in that location again.

THE CLOCK AND CANDLES GAME

The Clock and Candles Game is a ritual that tests one's bravery and curiosity by seeking truths revealed through the interplay of candlelight and time. It invites participants to pose questions to the darkness, as the clock ticks towards answers that may or may not wish to be known.

Prerequisites

Prepare a quiet room and cover all the windows, so any light can't go past.

Requirements

- A quiet room.
- An analog clock.
- Four candles.
- Matches or a lighter.
- A needle.
- Questions.

Warnings and Considerations

- Do not allow the game to exceed one hour in length under any circumstances.
- Do not ask questions that you might not want to know the answer for. Some things should remain unknown.

MIDNIGHT RITUALS

Step 1

Clear a large area on the floor in your room before midnight.

Gather all the required items to the playing space.

Step 2

Begin at exactly midnight by arranging the candles into a cross shape on the floor.

The candles need to be around 20 centimeters (about eight inches) apart.

Step 3

Put the analog clock in the middle of the cross.

Turn off the lights.

Sit near the clock and the candles and get ready to start the game.

Step 4

Starting with the northernmost and continuing clockwise, light each candle.

Step 5

Poke your finger with the needle until it bleeds.

Deposit one drop of your blood onto the center of the clock.

Step 6

With clear and respectful voice and wording, invite your correspondent(s).

Do it how you feel suitable, but be polite.

After speaking, wait

Step 7

If the candles remain lit, your invitation was not accepted.

Apologize, blow off the candles, turn on the light and leave the room.

Do not proceed this time, but you may try again another time.

If candle(s) goes out, your invitation is accepted.

One for each candle that was extinguished.

You may continue the ritual.

Step 8

Ask your questions aloud and watch the clock.

The hands of the clock will move to indicate the answer for your question.

See the picture at the end of this chapter to see how to read the answer

If the hands of the clock do not move, the spirits do not wish to answer.

Do not ask the same question again.

Step 9

Keep asking your questions until you have reached 10 questions.

Then, you must make a choice if you want to ask another set of 10 questions.

However, never under any circumstances allow the game to exceed one hour in total.

Step 10

If you wish to ask more questions, poke your finger with the needle again and deposit another drop of blood onto the center of the clock.

Repeat the steps from eight to ten.

Step 11

When you are done with your questions and need to end the game, you should thank your visitors for their time and ask them to leave.

Relight the candles that went out when the spirits arrived.

Step 12

If the candles remain lit, you may blow them out and clear your game area and leave the room.

If not, then keep repeating step 11 and pray it works.

How to read

Interpret each letter from the clock based on the position of the hour hand. Read a secondary letter, denoted as Z, from the position of the minute hand.

For instance, if the hour hand points to 6, the corresponding letter is K. Should the hour hand move closer to 5, the subsequent letter is I. Continue deciphering the message one letter at a time until both hands cease movement entirely.

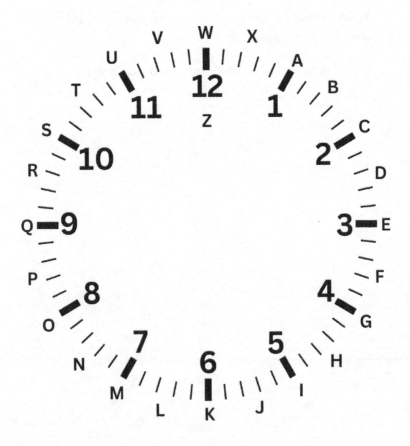

THE THREE WISHES RITUAL

The Three Wishes Ritual is an enigmatic and ancient practice that allows participants to make three wishes at a crossroads, a place believed to be filled with magical energy and potential. This ritual taps into deep-seated desires and offers a chance for them to manifest in mysterious ways.

Prerequisites

The night when the ritual is performed must be the full moon.

Requirements

- Three coins, each over ten years old
- A large field near a river
- Three wishes. One for love, one for money and one for health.

Warnings and Considerations

- After throwing the coins and turning away do not look back.
- Do not let anyone see you while performing the ritual, abort immediately if this happens.
- Do not fall asleep in the moonlight after completing this ritual.

Step 1

Put the coins in your pocket and wait until nightfall.

Travel to a large field near a river and begin.

Step 2

Stand anywhere in the field and make sure you are alone.

Step 3

Take the first coin from your pocket and hold it in your hand.

Concentrate on your first wish which is the wish for love.

Focus on it and visualize it in your mind really clearly. Say it aloud if it helps you.

While concentrating on your wish, throw the coin away as hard as you can.

Step 4

Take a breath and empty your mind.

Step 5

Take the second coin from your pocket and hold it in your hand.

Concentrate on your second wish which is the wish for money.

Again, focus on it and visualize it in your mind really clearly. Say it aloud if it helps you.

While concentrating on your wish, throw the coin away as hard as you can.

Step 6

Take a breath and empty your mind.

Step 7

Take the last coin from your pocket and hold it in your hand.

Concentrate on your third wish which is the wish for health.

Focus on it and visualize it in your mind really clearly. Once more say it aloud if it helps you.

While concentrating on your wish, throw the coin away as hard as you can.

Step 8

Take a breath and turn around facing away from the field.

Start walking away and don't look back.

Keep walking and whatever happens do not look back.

Step 9

The ritual is finished now, so all there is to do is to wait.

Soon your wish or wishes might come true if you wished hard enough.

TSUJI-URA

Tsuji-ura or the Fortune-Telling Game, is an ancient Japanese ritual that invites participants to learn their fate from a stranger at a crossroads. This mysterious practice blends curiosity with the supernatural, offering insights that may be as enlightening as they are unsettling.

Prerequisites

The ritual must be performed at night.

Requirements

- A comb.
- Something to cover your face.
- A crossroads.

Warnings and Considerations

- Do not uncover your face.

Step 1

Go to the crossroads.

Bring the comb and the item to cover your face.

Step 2

Strum the comb's teeth with your fingers three times.

Repeat the following sentence three times:

"Tsuji-ura. Tsuji-ura, grant me a true response".

Step 3

Wait patiently and watch your surroundings.

Step 4

If a stranger doesn't approach the crossroads the ritual has failed.

End the ritual and return home. You may try again another time.

If a stranger approaches the crossroads the ritual has succeeded.

You may continue the ritual.

Step 5

Immediately cover your face and do not let the stranger see you without the face cover.

Step 6

When the stranger is close, ask them to tell you your fortune, but be really polite.

If the stranger refuses or doesn't answer: Let them go and wait for another stranger to approach. Then repeat step 6.

If the stranger agrees to answer, proceed.

Step 7

Listen carefully to what the stranger tells you. Really close and carefully.

After they are done speaking, thank them and let them go.

While concentrating on your wish, throw the coin away as hard as you can.

Step 8

When the stranger has gone, return home and remove your face covering.

Don't let anyone follow you.

ABOUT THE AUTHOR

Sirius H. Dreamwalker is a seasoned explorer of the shadowy realms that lie at the fringes of human understanding. Originating from a family deeply entrenched in the study of arcane arts, Sirius has spent a lifetime curating and challenging the whispered legends of the night. Residing in the mist-shrouded hills of New England, Sirius draws inspiration from the eerie landscapes and rich folklore that surround him. Renowned for his meticulous research and compelling narrative style, Sirius brings a unique depth and authenticity to his exploration of paranormal rituals and games. Yearning to share his knowledge and experiences, Sirius has authored 'Midnight Rituals' to guide others through the chilling world of the unknown.

In his free time, Sirius enjoys stargazing, composing dark ambient music, and collecting rare occult books. Leveraging his background in folklore, Sirius hopes to connect with readers who are as fascinated by the supernatural as he is. Outside of writing, he advocates for the preservation of historical and haunted sites, believing that they hold keys to understanding the mysteries of our past. Venturing beyond the veil through his writings, Sirius invites his readers to peer into the depths of the eerie and the unexplained. Each of his works aims to challenge the boundary between the known and the unknown. You can discover more about his adventures into the paranormal on his website. Often found at the heart of a ghostly tale, Sirius continues to seek truths hidden in the shadows. Underneath the mystique of his pen name, Sirius H. Dreamwalker connects deeply with his readers through shared intrigue and curiosity.

Join Sirius as he delves into the world of the paranormal, inviting you to explore the eerie and the unknown through the pages of 'Midnight Rituals.' Inspired by the unseen, his writings illuminate the darkest corners of folklore and fear. Never far from a haunted locale, Sirius seeks inspiration in the quiet whispers of history. Guided by a lifetime of curiosity, Sirius H. Dreamwalker invites you to uncover the mysteries that lurk in the shadows with 'Midnight Rituals.'